"I have k[nown]... have adm[ired]... wondered how he was ab[le]... knew was a terribly broken family to accomplish what he has as a professional, as a father, and as a Christian. This book is a practical roadmap to success. Individually, you may or may not view the steps Chris took as groundbreaking, but combined they are powerful. As I read I noticed I had already incorporated a number of his concepts, and now I'm carefully considering the others. By the time you read this, I promise each of them will be added to my list!"

> — **RON JOELSON**, former Chief Investment Offer of Northwestern Mutual; author of *An Unexpected Journey into the Heart of God*

"When I met Chris Koon as a young man, I felt his energy and knew he had discipline because of his running. His personal growth through trials and tribulations has created a purpose in him to inform, challenge, and give others the choice to grow and accomplish their dreams. This book is his story. It's a great one!"

> — **John Qualy**, former Managing Partner of Northwestern Mutual

"Over the years I have watched Chris Koon set and achieve nearly impossible goals time and time again. Working alongside Chris, witnessing his incredible journey, and seeing the positive impact he has on his family and career, has been a privilege. The world shines brighter with his presence. *Unleashing Potential* is a chronicle of his journey, infused with insights that can only come from someone who lives and breathes personal growth and altruism. This is not just a book; it's a mirror of Chris's depth and passion—an invaluable guide for anyone aspiring to make meaningful progress, professionally or personally."

— **Michelle Magner**, Partner at Socium Advisors

"In *Unleashing Potential*, Chris packs a ton of valuable insights into how anyone can take small steps toward exponential growth. Over the years, through Chris's inspiration and financial prowess, he has helped me become financially free and helped my business thrive"

— **David Meggs**, Co-Founder & CEO, AXSYS Capital

UNLEASHING
POTENTIAL

A BLUEPRINT
— FOR —
EXCEPTIONAL GROWTH

Christopher O. Koon

Copyright © 2024 by Christopher O. Koon

Unleashing Potential: A Blueprint for Exceptional Growth

All rights reserved. No part of this publication may be reproduced, distributed or transmitted in any form or by any means, including photocopying, recording, or other electronic or mechanical methods, without the prior written permission of the publisher, except in the case of brief quotations embodied in critical reviews and certain other noncommercial uses permitted by copyright law. Neither the author nor the publisher assumes any responsibility or liability whatsoever on behalf of the consumer or reader of this material. Any perceived slight of any individual or organization is purely unintentional. The resources in this book are provided for informational purposes only and should not be used to replace the specialized training and professional judgment of a healthcare or mental health care professional. Neither the author nor the publisher can be held responsible for the use of the information provided within this book. Please, always consult a trained professional before making any decision regarding treatment of yourself or others.

Paperback ISBN: 979-8-9899476-0-7
eBook ISBN: 979-8-9899476-1-4

TO THE GREATEST GIFTS IN MY LIFE:

My wife **Lisa Rose**
My daughter **Ava Rose**
My son **Berkley**
My son **Gunnar**

CONTENTS

Foreword ix
Introduction 1

UNLIKELY SUCCESS
My Story from Box Spring to Breakthrough
3

THE POWER OF VISION
Goals, Letters, and the Right People
15

PEAK PERFORMANCE
Four Habits for Extraordinary Success
31

FORCE FOR GOOD
Making a Difference through Generosity
45

GROUNDED IN GRACE
The Role of Faith in My Life
53

FOREWORD

EVERYONE LOVES a good underdog story about overcoming the odds, and that's exactly what you're going to get when you read *Unleashing Potential*. More than that, you're going to get a game plan you can use to overcome the challenges you face in your own life too.

Chris Koon embodies the fight and the freedom of individual choice. He overcame a challenging childhood and his own demons as a young man. After he turned his life around, Chris optimized his talents and quickly rose through the ranks to become a successful top 1 percent wealth advisor for Northwestern Mutual.

Without a doubt, my life would be much different today if it were not for his kindness. Early in my financial services career, Chris became a mentor and friend who went out of his way to help me. When I was a new advisor at Northwestern Mutual, Chris took me under his tutelage even though I wasn't on his team. He helped me achieve success out of the goodness of his heart and earned no commissions from the deals I closed.

When I decided to make the move into performance coaching, Chris was also there every step of the way. He booked some of my early speaking engagements and influenced me with several concepts that became part of my foundational messages to audiences.

His service to me and his ongoing kindness to others is why he remains an integral part of my inner circle to this day.

As you'll read in these pages, I'm only one of many people Chris has helped over the years. Until now, his coaching, mentorship, and fellowship have only reached a fraction of the people who could benefit from his accumulated knowledge and wisdom. But *Unleashing Potential* changes all that. For the first time, Chris has laid out the tactics and strategies he has used for more than two decades to overcome his past and become a man trusted by many for some of the most important decisions in their lives.

I have used many of these same strategies for years. They are portable, timeless, and easy to understand by design. They are also practical and proven, much more than untested theories from someone who has never had any real skin in the game. And Chris has laid them out in plain language so that no matter what your station in life, you can grasp their meaning and use them to benefit yourself.

Endorsing *Unleashing Potential* is one small way I can repay Chris's significant contributions to my life while at the same time turning you on to his compelling story. More importantly, when you're done with this book, you'll have many of the tools you need to craft a better life for yourself and those you care about.

If you can achieve that, then Chris's words will have the desired impact he has always hoped for.

Thank you, Chris, for sharing your story and insights.

BEN NEWMAN, *USA Today* Top 5 Performance Coach and *Wall Street Journal* bestselling author of *UNCOMMON Leadership* and *The STANDARD*

INTRODUCTION

THE FIRST TIME I got drunk, I was seven years old.

My dad, mom, brother, sister, and I lived in St. Louis, home of Budweiser. We were all steeped in a culture where alcohol was a constant companion. Whether it was at my dad's apartment across town or with my mom's friends, drinks were always being served.

From a young age, I saw alcohol as a way to escape. I was generally a shy kid, but when I drank, I was the life of the party. And I couldn't get enough.

By the time I was twelve years old, I was regularly drinking and getting drunk. In high school I learned to "shotgun a beer" (when you stab the side of a can and guzzle it) in one second.

By the time I was in college, I stepped things up and started doing cocaine too.

Fast-forward to when I was twenty years old. I was a college dropout, barely employed, living on a box spring and mattress in my older brother's living room.

From here my story could have turned very dark. Honestly, I wasn't far from being homeless or even dying of an overdose.

But thankfully my story took a turn for the better. By God's grace and through the love of some wonderful people, things started to turn around.

In fact, in just two years I went from that box spring in my brother's living room to being sober, physically fit, and making a high six-figure income. I went on to marry my beautiful wife, Lisa Rose, and have a wonderful family.

My story is one of unlikely success.

How did it happen? This book not only tells you how; it gives you the principles that helped me experience more success than I ever dreamed possible—in every area of life.

I can't wait to share it all with you. Here we go!

UNLIKELY SUCCESS
MY STORY FROM BOX SPRING TO BREAKTHROUGH

I WAS BORN to Tom and Mimi Koon on March 7, 1969, in the bustling city of St. Louis, Missouri.

My grandfather had done very well, so my parents enjoyed a sizable inheritance. When I was four years old, I went to a pre-kindergarten school called The Wilson School. It was a beautiful place, and the teachers were amazing.

But if you were listening to the soundtrack of my life, here is when you'd hear a loud SCRAAAAATCH! across the record.

In short, my parents divorced, and that meant my mom, brother, sister, and I had to move to a smaller house across town.

Mom took me to a new pre-K school called Jack and Jill, and I knew the instant I saw the place that I didn't want to be there.

Memories of Jack and Jill are still vivid in my mind. The school was located on a busy street, a stark contrast to the serene neighborhood of The Wilson School. I remember the day my mom drove me there in our light blue wood-panel Plymouth station wagon. The school was surrounded by a massive fence. As we approached the entrance, a sense of dread washed over me. The place felt cold, dark, and unwelcoming. I recall the vast space inside with its gleaming floors, reflecting the overhead lights in an eerie glow.

My first day there was a nightmare. As my mom left, I clung to the fence, tears streaming down my face, pleading with her not to abandon me in this unfamiliar place. The feeling of being trapped, of being in a place where I didn't belong, was overwhelming.

A Glimmer of Hope?

I was so thankful to get out of there and go to first grade at Maryland School. My teacher, Mrs. Jones, had kind eyes and a gentle demeanor. But about six months in, just as I was feeling settled, Mrs. Jones pulled me out into the hallway. I can still hear the echoes of the door closing and our footsteps on the hard floor.

Mrs. Jones broke the news that because I wasn't learning as quickly as other students, I would be placed in a different room, one with kids ranging from first to sixth grade. It felt like another blow, another reminder that I was different.

This "special class" was located past the gym and up a flight of stairs—where everyone else could forget we existed. It felt like a broom closet. Inside, the environment was challenging, to say the least. I remember one of the older students, Mark, who had a reputation for aggressive behavior. Rumor had it, he had punched a couple of teachers.

I went from the nurturing environment of Mrs. Jones to one of profound stress and fear. The worst part was the other students teased me with labels like "flunker."

Mia

Despite the challenges, there were moments of respite. My grandmother, Mia, was a pillar of strength in my life, especially during the tumultuous times following my parents' divorce. We lived in a smaller house after the separation, and my mom, working as a travel agent, did her best to provide for us. But it was my grandmother who often stepped in to offer additional support, sending extra money and ensuring we had what we needed.

Her generosity wasn't just financial; she provided emotional support too. Every summer I visited her beautiful place in East Hampton, New York. Those visits were a stark contrast to my daily life, offering a glimpse into a world of luxury and comfort. I was the youngest of her sixteen grandkids, and I always felt I held a special place in her heart.

My grandmother was not just a doting figure; she was formidable. In a time when many women were relegated to the background, she stood out as a force to be reckoned with. She held her own and was respected by all who knew her. Her resilience and determination were evident in every story she told and every piece of advice she shared. She was, in many ways, ahead of her time, challenging societal norms and expectations. Her strength was not just in her words but in her actions, and she served as a role model for me in countless ways.

Father

My parents' divorce opened a significant void in my life, particularly concerning my relationship with my father. I vividly recall the day I was informed that my dad had gotten married to a woman named Beth. Realizing I wasn't invited to the ceremony, I ran to my room and cried into my pillow.

Our interactions with him became sporadic. Occasionally he'd pick us up, and we'd go to Steak 'n Shake for dinner. A few times we stayed the night at his apartment.

The holidays were particularly telling. We'd exchange gifts at my dad's in the morning and then were quickly returned to my mom so that he and Beth could leave for her family's celebrations. It felt like we were an afterthought.

It wasn't all terrible. There were moments of connection, but these moments were fleeting, overshadowed by the challenges of his alcoholism and our strained relationship. His struggles with drinking were evident, and while I knew he loved me, the consistency and depth of our relationship were lacking.

New Discoveries

Growing up in St. Louis, the home of Budweiser, alcohol was a significant part of our family culture. From a young age, I was exposed to drinking.

When I was seven, I followed along with my mom when she and her friends went golfing. I jumped into one of the golf carts with her friend. It was just natural for me to sneak beers as we went along. I kept drinking until I found myself passed out in my mom's car.

I was a hyperactive, unruly kid, so my parents sent me to a military school in eighth grade. It was an experience straight out of *An Officer and a Gentleman*.

I benefited from the structure, but the academics were too hard for me. This is when, after being tested, I was diagnosed as dyslexic. I would read the same line over and over again without understanding it. If you handed me a book, it just seemed like a crossword puzzle.

My First Love

One highlight from my childhood was running. My older brother, Tom, noticed I was a hyperactive kid, so he found some running shoes in the school locker room and gave them to me when I was nine years old. I remember putting on those shoes and just flying. I loved running.

Not only did I love it, I was really good at it. I started entering 5Ks and 10Ks and not just doing well but actually winning. This was against the backdrop of not doing very well in school and always being made to feel less than. All of a sudden here was something I was really good at. It was a huge lift for me.

One memory stands out in particular. I entered a 10K called the Stadium Run when I was ten years old. So did long-distance runner Craig Virgin. Craig had won five state championships in high school and qualified as an Olympic runner three times. He likely would have won the gold medal in 1980, but President Carter boycotted the Olympics that year. Craig Virgin was my idol.

So off we go on this 6.2-mile race. With about a mile and a half left, I was in first place when some spectators came up beside me in their cars and told me that Craig Virgin was coming fast. I started turning around and looking for him. If I had stayed focused, I probably would have beat him. He ended up passing me toward the end of the race, and I came in second. Keep in mind I was ten years old at the time; Craig was twenty-four.

That was the aha moment when I realized how fast I was.

High School, College, and Beyond

I completed eighth grade in military school, but the academics were too challenging for me to continue. My parents sent me to Forman Boarding School in Litchfield, Connecticut, because they had a good track record of working with kids with dyslexia. It was a positive experience, but the hole inside me was always being filled with alcohol and other substances. By the time I was fifteen, drinking excessively was a weekend ritual, and I also started smoking weed. I recall summers working at a gas station and partying hard.

After graduating from high school, I went to Marshall University in Huntington, West Virginia, because they had a program for students with learning differences. I did well my first year, but by the second year I went deep into drugs. Partying was all that mattered to me. Everything else went out the window.

I started experimenting with drugs, notably cocaine. This led to severe panic attacks, which became a daily ordeal. I felt trapped in a cycle of despair, questioning if I'd ever feel normal again.

I didn't make it long into my second year of college before I dropped out. I found myself at a Greyhound bus stop with a twelve-pack of beer to deal with my anxiety, waiting for a bus to take me back to St. Louis to live with my brother. I was there only a short period of time before moving to Jacksonville, Florida, where my mom lived at the time. I got a job working on a golf course. There, I was surrounded by successful individuals, which only highlighted my deteriorating state. The fun I once associated with drinking was now overshadowed by problems and consequences.

After a period in Florida, I returned to St. Louis, where my struggles with alcoholism reached a breaking point. The fun had turned to despair, and I found myself yearning for a way out.

So there I was. Twenty years old. A college dropout living with my brother, drinking from the time I got up until the time I went to bed.

Then one night changed my life. I was coming home from my bar backing job, and the road was familiar. I took the exit, the same one I'd taken many times before, but this time, everything went blank. I passed out behind the wheel. The next thing I knew, half my car was perched on top of a concrete barrier. It was a miracle I didn't flip over or worse. I'm convinced God saved my life.

The officer on the scene could have thrown the book at me, but for some reason, he didn't. I was a mess, a good talker maybe, but still a mess.

I managed to convince him I wasn't as drunk as I probably was, rattling off excuses, trying to downplay the danger I'd put myself and others in.

I sat there with the flashing lights painting the night in stark strokes of red and blue. My heart was pounding, a mix of adrenaline and fear. The officer's words were firm but not unkind, "You're lucky to be alive, son." And he was right. I somehow eased the car off the barrier and drove back to my place. The reality of what could have happened weighed heavily on me.

Once home, I stared at the damaged car, the bent wheel a stark reminder of my recklessness. I couldn't shake the image of my car teetering on the edge of that barrier. It was a metaphor for my life at that point—always on the brink, a constant balancing act between chaos and the daily grind.

That night, alone in the silence of my apartment, the buzz of the near-miss still in my ears, I knew something had to change. I couldn't keep flirting with disaster. The officer's mercy was a gift, an unexpected chance to right my course before it was too late. It was time to face the music, to confront the demons that drove me to drink and drive and nearly throw it all away.

I made a promise to myself as I lay in bed, staring at the ceiling. No more close calls, no more excuses. It was the moment I truly understood that if I didn't turn things around, I might not get another chance. That accident wasn't just a scare; it was a lifeline thrown to me in the dark waters of my life. And I was ready to grab hold.

Getting Sober

I had been to some Alcoholics Anonymous meetings during my boarding school days, but I wasn't really committed to being sober back then. Now I started going to meetings in earnest, and eventually, thanks to my grandmother's generosity, I enrolled in Edgewood, a residential treatment center.

When I entered rehab, I was at a crossroads in my life. I remember sitting in that treatment center, listening intently as the leader, Father Martin, spoke. He said something that struck me hard: "One in thirty-two people are going to make it." Looking around the room, with probably forty of us in there, those odds seemed daunting. But in that moment, I made a decision. I thought to myself, "I'm owning this chair. I'm the one." I felt it deep in my bones. I was ready to do whatever it took.

My thirty days in rehab were a period of intense self-reflection and surrender. I learned to get on my knees and pray to God every day, to work through the steps of Alcoholics Anonymous, and to believe in a power greater than myself. It was a spiritual journey—one that required me to confront my addiction head-on and to start the process of healing.

After rehab, I moved to a halfway house in Granite City, Illinois. It was a challenging environment, right next to a bar, constantly reminding me of my past life. I even had a bottle of Jack Daniels in my car, a gift for my brother. The temptation was there, but my resolve was stronger. I didn't want to drink anymore. That bottle was a test, and I was determined to pass it.

My First Real Jobs

After rehab, I started rebuilding my life from the ground up. My first job was painting, a humble but honest start. I got the job through a friend, and it lasted about three months. Then I moved on to a grocery store job, which I held for another few months. These jobs might seem small, but they were crucial for me. They kept me grounded and gave me a sense of purpose.

During this time, I was also deeply committed to the AA program. I attended meetings religiously, sometimes going to more than one a day. I had great sponsors and was fully invested in the program. I knew that if I stayed focused and worked the steps, God would take care of me.

A guy in the AA program offered me a job selling secondary steel, paying me $1,000 a month. One memory I have from this period is getting a Mazda DLC for $700. It didn't have a starter, so I had to pop start it anytime I went anywhere. I didn't have much, but I was building confidence.

A year later another buddy hired me in the trucking business, where I worked for another year. It was during my time in the trucking business when I bought a life insurance policy from a guy at Northwestern Mutual, and I remember being inspired by the life he led.

About two and a half years after rehab, a friend referred me to a position in the financial services industry. This was a significant turning point. I entered this new career with just a thousand dollars to my name, but I was rich in determination and drive.

The transition wasn't easy, but I applied the same discipline and commitment that I learned in AA to my new career. I followed the Granum system at Northwestern Mutual, a structured approach that promised success if followed diligently. This system, much like the AA program, provided a framework that guided my actions and decisions.

It worked. In my first year I made it into what's called the Million Dollar Round Table, an association of the top life insurance and financial services professionals in the world. Less than half of one percent of people in this industry achieve this in their first year.

Since then, I've been very fortunate to experience not just financial success, but a deeper, more fulfilling life. For the rest of this book, I'd like to share some habits and principles that have had a huge impact on my life. If you follow these in your own life, I'm confident they'll help you unleash your potential!

THE POWER OF VISION
GOALS, LETTERS, AND THE RIGHT PEOPLE

FROM A YOUNG AGE, I felt a sense of direction, a nudge toward something greater, even when the path wasn't clear. As a child, I had glimpses of a vision for my life, but these were often clouded by the chaos of my circumstances. My journey to developing a vision for my life wasn't linear; it was filled with ups and downs, clarity and confusion.

During my darkest days, when alcohol and drugs consumed my life, my vision was completely obscured. I lived day to day, moment to moment, without any thought for the future. It was a time of profound lostness—a stark contrast to the clarity and purpose I found later.

The sport of running was an important part of my development. It taught me discipline and resilience, and it gave me a sense of achievement, laying the foundation for the vision I would build for my life. But my relationship with vision truly began to develop during my recovery.

Recovery wasn't just about getting sober; it was about envisioning a life that was radically different from the one I was living. This vision became a crucial tool for my transformation. Vision helps you push beyond your comfort zone and sometimes push back from where you came from.

As I entered the financial services industry, my vision started to crystallize. Initially, I didn't have grand ambitions of achieving extraordinary success. My focus was on working hard and following the systems in place. But as I progressed, my vision expanded. I began to see the potential for not just financial success, but a life of true fulfillment and purpose.

In this chapter we'll explore how even a fuzzy vision can guide you, the importance of setting goals, the power of writing a letter from your future self, and the impact of connecting with successful people. These are the practices that helped me refine and realize my vision, and I believe they can do the same for you.

Embracing the Fuzziness of Vision

In the journey of life, having a crystal-clear vision from the start is rare. More often, our vision starts as a blur. This was certainly true for me. There were times when my vision was nothing more than a faint outline, a hazy idea of where I wanted to go.

But here's the key: even a fuzzy vision can guide you. It's like walking through a fog—you might not see the destination, but you can take one step at a time. Each step brings a little more clarity, a little more understanding of where you're headed.

During my early days in the financial services industry, my vision wasn't fully formed. I knew I wanted success, but what that looked like in detail, I couldn't say. However, I committed to learning and doing my best. I embraced the uncertainty and kept moving forward.

As I progressed, my vision started to become clear. The experiences I gained, the failures I encountered, and the successes I celebrated all contributed to refining my vision. I learned that commitment to growth and a willingness to step into the unknown are crucial in clarifying your vision.

It's okay if your vision isn't perfect from the start. What's important is your commitment to learning and improving. As you grow and evolve, so will your vision. It's a dynamic process, one that requires patience, perseverance, and an open mind.

In the following sections, we'll delve into practical strategies like setting goals and writing letters from your future self, which can help bring your vision into sharper focus. But for now, know that it's perfectly normal for your vision to start out a little fuzzy. Embrace it, and trust that with time and effort, it will become clearer.

Going after $10,000

In my life and career, setting goals has always been a straightforward yet effective practice. Whether these goals are personal, professional, or financial, the key is to start jotting them down. It could be anything from planning great trips with your spouse to setting new client goals in your business.

For me, in the financial services industry, my goals varied from sales goals and new client targets, to premium goals and identifying qualified prospects. On a personal front, it might be as simple as starting to exercise, aiming to lose weight, or deciding to read more books.

One of the most important goals I set early in my career involved a clear financial target. I was new to the industry, still figuring out the ropes, and I knew I needed a concrete, measurable objective to strive for. I decided on a goal of generating $10,000 in premium per month. This number wasn't just plucked from thin air; it was calculated. I knew this amount would not only cover my living expenses but also establish a strong foundation in my career. It was ambitious, especially for someone just starting out, but that was the point. I wanted a goal that pushed me out of my comfort zone.

To achieve this, I broke down the goal into weekly and daily activities. I figured out how many calls I needed to make, how many meetings I needed to set up, and how many proposals I needed to present each week to hit this target. Every morning I reviewed these mini-goals, and every evening I evaluated my progress. It wasn't easy. There were days when I felt I was fighting an uphill battle, but the clarity of that goal kept me focused.

I remember vividly the first month I hit that $10,000 mark. It was exhilarating. It wasn't just about the money; it was about proving to myself that I could set a significant goal and achieve it. This accomplishment laid the foundation for my future successes. More importantly, it instilled in me a deep belief in the power of setting clear, actionable goals. It taught me that when you break down a big goal into manageable steps, and consistently work toward it, achieving it is not a matter of if, but when.

Tips for Effective Goal Setting

Following are some goal-setting rules of thumb that have worked well for me, and I recommend them to you:

- **Keep It Simple:** Goals don't have to be overcomplicated. They can be as straightforward as calling your mom once a week or joining a book club. What matters is that they resonate with you.
- **Write Them Down:** There's a unique power in writing your goals. It transforms them

from thoughts to tangible objectives. This act alone can set the stage for achieving them.
- **Review Regularly:** I recommend reading your goals twice daily—once in the morning and once at night. This practice helps keep them at the forefront of your mind and aligns your daily actions with your long-term objectives.
- **Personalize Your Goals:** Remember, goals are deeply personal and will differ for each individual. Your goals should reflect *your* aspirations and help guide *your* actions.
- **Connect Your Goals with Vision:** Goals are the stepping stones toward your larger vision. They should align with where you see yourself going, in both the short and the long term.

In essence, goal setting helps you identify what you want to achieve and then methodically work toward it. It's a blend of aspiration and action, all tailored to your unique journey.

Mail Call: A Letter from Your Future Self

One of the most inspiring practices I've embraced is writing a letter from my future self to my current self. This is a powerful way to visualize success and personal growth.

The concept is simple yet profound: you position yourself in the future, having already accomplished your dreams, and write back to your present self. Doing this helps you detail the life you want to live, the challenges you want to overcome, and the joys you want to experience.

Imagine writing from a point in time where you've achieved not just your professional ambitions but also personal milestones. As motivational speaker Jim Rohn says, "Success is something you attract by the person you become."

For instance, picture yourself several years from now, having achieved key milestones in your career. Maybe you've grown your business beyond your wildest dreams or achieved that elusive work-life balance you've always strived for. Don't stop there. Envision the quality of your personal life—the relationships you've nurtured, the personal goals you've achieved, and how you've grown as an individual.

This letter should be a narrative of success. As you write, let the emotions flow—the pride, the satisfaction, the joy. Doing this activity solidifies your vision for the future and instills a sense of hope and direction. Try it!

Your future self has a lot to tell you about the victories, the hard-earned wisdom, and the person you've become. So grab your laptop or take out a pen and paper. Let your future self speak to you. It's a conversation that could change the course of your life.

Recreating My Letter

I looked and looked for the letter my future self wrote to me early in my career. Alas, I couldn't find it, but I've done my best to recreate it below:

Dear Chris,

Greetings from the future! I'm writing to you from a place of accomplishment and profound personal satisfaction. It's been an incredible journey, and I want to share some of the highlights to give you a glimpse of your future.

Your professional life has exceeded your wildest dreams. Remember when you set your sights on making a significant impact in the financial services industry? Well, you've done that and more. You've grown your business beyond what you thought possible, helping countless individuals and families secure their financial futures. Your dedication and hard work have paid off, and you're recognized as a leader in your field.

But the good news goes beyond professional success. You met a beautiful woman, both inside and out, and the two of you are growing both as individuals and as a couple. You've even got a little one on the way!

Your commitment to personal growth has been unwavering. You've stayed sober by going back again and again to your Creator. You're continuously learning and evolving. The challenges you faced, the obstacles you overcame, they've all contributed to the person you've become—resilient, compassionate, and wise.

Most importantly, you've remained humble and grateful throughout your journey. You've used your success to give back, to mentor others starting their paths, and to make a positive difference in the world. The community respects and admires you not just for your professional achievements but for the kind of person you've become.

So keep pushing forward, Chris! You've got this! The road might seem daunting at times, but every step you take is a step closer to this incredible future. Stay true to your dreams, maintain your integrity, and never lose sight of what truly matters.

With admiration and encouragement,
Future Chris

Ready to write a letter from your future self? Go for it!

The Rolls Royce Ritual

Sid Freeman, one of the greatest life insurance salesmen and a professional acquaintance of mine, had a unique method of manifesting his dreams. Our connection came through his son-in-law, Ian Freeman, who works at Northwestern Mutual. Sid's approach to achieving goals was as unconventional as it was inspiring.

Sid had a dream to own a Rolls Royce. Rather than just dreaming about it, he took an extraordinary step. Every week for a year, he visited a Rolls Royce dealership. He would sit in the car, feel the leather, and immerse himself in the experience of owning it. Sid wasn't just thinking about the car; he was living the experience in advance. Then, a year to the day later, he returned to the dealership and bought the Rolls Royce.

This story resonates deeply with the practice of writing a letter from your future self. Just like Sid's regular visits to the Rolls Royce, the letter is a way to immerse yourself in the reality of your future achievements. It's about creating a vivid, tangible connection to the future you aspire to.

When you write from your future self, you're doing more than just setting goals or daydreaming about what could be. You are actively living in that future success, feeling the emotions, and experiencing the achievements as if they were already real. It's a powerful method to bridge the gap between your present and the future you're working toward.

So as you embark on this exercise, remember Sid and his Rolls Royce. Let his story inspire you to not just envision your future but to feel and experience it in your present. This approach can transform your goals from mere aspirations into lived realities.

Gleaning from Giants

One of the most transformative practices in my journey has been connecting with successful people. Doing so helps you surround yourself with individuals who have achieved what you aspire to and learning from their experiences. Insurance legend Charlie "Tremendous" Jones said, "You will be the same person in five years as you are today, except for the people you meet and the books you read."

It was early in my career when I had an encounter that reshaped my entire approach to connecting with successful people. I was still finding my footing in the world of insurance sales, a field where success hinges on your ability to connect with people from all walks of life. That's when Jack Musgrave came into the picture. Musgrave wasn't just any client; he was a titan in the legal field, known for his sharp intellect and formidable presence in the courtroom. To a young professional like me, he was both inspiring and more than a little intimidating!

Our paths crossed in an unexpected way. I had recently sold an insurance policy to Musgrave's daughter, a straightforward transaction that took an interesting turn when I was asked to meet with Jack Musgrave himself. Jack wanted to make sure his daughter wasn't making a poor decision.

The prospect of meeting someone of his stature sent a wave of nerves through me. I remember meticulously preparing for the meeting, going over every possible question he might ask. As the day approached, I realized this was more than just a business meeting; it was a golden opportunity to learn from someone who had reached the pinnacle of success in his field.

Walking into Musgrave's office, I was struck by the sheer aura of the man. His accomplishments lined the walls, yet there was a simplicity about him that was disarming. As we spoke, I was surprised by his approachability and genuine interest in the policy details. He listened intently, asked insightful questions, and in those moments I felt a shift in my own perception. Here was a man who had achieved so much, yet he respected my work and treated me as an equal. That interaction taught me a powerful lesson: no matter how high someone may rise, at the core, we are all people, striving and learning.

That meeting with Musgrave left an indelible mark on me. I left his office with a newfound confidence, a belief that I could hold my own in conversations with even the most successful individuals. From then on, I approached my career with a different mindset. I learned that connecting with successful people means engaging with them, learning from their experiences, and taking those lessons to heart. Jack Musgrave may never know it, but that one meeting played a pivotal role in shaping the professional I am today.

Approaching an Icon

There's another story that stands out vividly in my mind. It's about Fred Palmer, an individual I encountered early in my career. Mr. Palmer worked for Peabody Coal, a significant player in the coal industry. He was someone who clearly had considerable wealth, evident from his habit of buying new $100,000 cars every few months. Our paths crossed because we worked in the same building; my office was on the tenth floor while Peabody Coal was on the ninth.

I remember one snowy day seeing Mr. Palmer drive into the parking lot in his Porsche 911. That moment sparked something in me. I started making it a point to greet him in the mornings. "Good morning, Mr. Palmer," I'd say, "looking sharp!" I seized these brief interactions to start conversations. It was my way of slowly building a connection.

One day, motivated by the confidence I had built from our previous interactions, I decided to take a leap. I called Mr. Palmer, mentioning that I saw him driving his Porsche in the snow and used that as a conversation starter. I was upfront with him—I told him about my work with Northwestern Mutual and expressed my eagerness to meet successful people like him. I was new in the business, and I believed I had valuable ideas to share. It was a bold move, but it resulted in an appointment with Mr. Palmer in his office.

The meeting with Mr. Palmer was a defining moment for me. Although I never did business with him, the experience was invaluable. Being in the presence of someone so successful, in his environment, was inspiring. It taught me the importance of stepping out of my comfort zone and the impact of being around successful people. That encounter gave me a significant confidence boost and reinforced the idea that successful people are approachable. Building connections with them can lead to unexpected opportunities and growth.

How to Connect with Successful People

Here's how I approached this practice:

- **Identify Influential People**: Start by identifying people in your community or industry whom you admire and respect. These could be leaders in your field, successful entrepreneurs, or anyone whose success resonates with your goals.
- **Reach Out and Connect:** Don't hesitate to reach out. This could be through email, a phone call, or even a casual conversation if you happen to meet them at an event or a common place like a gym. The key is to make that initial contact.
- **Be Curious about Them:** Once you've made contact, engage them from a posture of curiosity. Ask them about their journey, the challenges they faced, and the lessons

they learned. Be genuinely interested in their story without any hidden agenda.
- **Learn from Their Wisdom:** Often, successful people can offer insights and advice that you might not find in books or online. Ask them what they wish they had known at your age or in your stage of career development. This can provide invaluable guidance for your own path.
- **Build Genuine Relationships:** It's important to approach these connections with sincerity. This isn't about what you can get out of the relationship, but about building a genuine connection. Offer your own insights and help where you can.
- **Apply Their Lessons to Your Life:** Finally, take the wisdom and lessons you've gained from these interactions and apply them to your own journey. It's one thing to hear advice; it's another to put it into action in your own life.

Connecting with successful people has been a game changer for me. People always talk about networking, but this is more than that. Connecting with people you admire is about learning from those who have already walked the path you're on. Their experiences can light the way for your own success journey. I encourage you to be bold and reach out to someone today!

Vision Realized

As we wrap up this chapter on the power of vision, I want to leave you with a final thought. Vision isn't just about seeing where you want to go; it's about believing you can get there. Vision involves blending the practicality of goal-setting and the inspiration of dreaming big.

The path to achieving your vision is not always straightforward. It's filled with challenges, uncertainties, and moments of doubt. But it's also lined with opportunities, learnings, and moments of triumph. Like my encounters with Jack Musgrave and Fred Palmer, each experience you have, each person you meet, adds a piece to your vision puzzle. They help clarify your path, refine your goals, and ultimately, shape the person you become.

I urge you to embrace your vision, no matter how fuzzy it is at the start. Let it guide you, inspire you, and push you beyond your limits.

Write that letter from your future self.

Write down your ambitious goals.

Connect with people who inspire you.

Your vision is a powerful tool, not just for guiding your path but for transforming your life. Trust in it, work toward it, and watch as it unfolds into a reality beyond your wildest dreams.

PEAK PERFORMANCE
FOUR HABITS FOR EXTRAORDINARY SUCCESS

SUCCESS, IN MY EXPERIENCE, is less about inherent talent or luck and more about the deliberate practice of transformative habits. The four habits I'll cover in this chapter have been like the steady rhythm of a drummer, setting the tempo and keeping me in sync with my goals.

These small, daily practices accumulate to create significant, lasting impacts in all facets of life. Here we go!

Habit #1: Fitness as a Foundation

Exercise and physical fitness have always been integral to my daily routine, not just for maintaining my health, but for fostering a mindset that primes me for success. My day begins early, often around 4:00 AM. This early start allows me to engage in a physical workout that sets the tone for the rest of my day.

Getting to the gym by 4:30 AM for a class that starts at 5:00, I go for it in a rigorous workout. I want to stress the workout is more than just physical exercise; it's a mental preparation for the day ahead. Starting my day with exercise not only boosts my energy levels but also provides me with mental clarity and a sense of achievement. It's a time when I can think about my day, plan my activities, and set my intentions.

Over the years my exercise routines have varied. I've run marathons, worked with personal trainers, and participated in community fitness programs like Orange Theory. What has remained constant is my commitment to staying active, which I believe is crucial for anyone aiming for peak performance in their professional and personal lives. Exercise is a great stress reliever and a source of inspiration. It's where I can daydream, envision, and mentally prepare for the impact I want to make each day.

Physical fitness helps me stay in shape, of course, but it's more than that. It improves the quality of my life. Being fit allows me to engage in activities that are physically demanding yet immensely rewarding. Whether it's participating in challenging events or simply being able to play actively with my kids, fitness enhances my life experience. It makes me feel alive and connected to the world around me.

In my view, the habit of exercise is perhaps the most important one you can develop. It brings longevity, vitality, and a quality of life that's hard to match. Even if it doesn't add years to your life, the quality of those years is vastly improved. Letting your body remain inactive is a missed opportunity to experience life to its fullest.

So for anyone reading this, I encourage you to find a form of exercise you enjoy. It could be anything from walking and hiking to more intense workouts. The key is movement and being part of a community that motivates you to be your best self. Here are a few practical tips to get started:

- **Start with Something Manageable:** If you're new to exercise, begin with small, achievable goals. This could be a short walk each day, a few minutes of stretching in the morning, or a beginner's yoga class. The aim is to build a habit that you can gradually expand upon.
- **Mix It Up:** Variety is the spice of life, and this holds true for exercise too. Try different activities to keep things interesting and to work out different muscle groups. This could mean alternating between cardio, strength training, and flexibility exercises throughout the week.
- **Set Regular Goals:** Setting short-term and long-term fitness goals can keep you motivated. Whether it's increasing the distance you can run, the weight you can lift, or the number of push-ups you can do,

having clear targets gives you something to pursue.
- **Find a Workout Buddy or Join a Group:** Exercising with a friend or joining a fitness group can significantly boost your motivation. It's not just about the exercise; it's also about the social interaction and support that comes with being part of a fitness community. I've met some of my best customers and business partners while exercising!

Remember, the most important thing is to find an activity that you enjoy and that fits into your lifestyle. It's not really about pushing yourself to extremes but about building a sustainable and enjoyable fitness routine that enhances your life.

Habit #2: Cultivating a Growth Mindset

Alongside physical fitness, mindset work is a pillar of my daily routine that has been crucial in shaping my path to success. Understanding and nurturing the mind is as important as caring for the body. For me, this involves a continuous process of mental exercise and self-education, a practice that has been both challenging and rewarding.

I used to get frustrated when I heard people say, "Knowledge is power." I assumed dyslexia made it impossible for me to pursue knowledge.

Overcoming this obstacle wasn't easy, but I learned to feed my mind through various mediums, from listening to podcasts to watching informative videos. Each of these activities expands my understanding and perspectives, which is essential for personal and professional growth.

My approach to mindset work is about intentionally choosing what information I consume. Being selective about the content that enters my mind is as important as the food that nourishes my body. I focus on materials that inspire, educate, and challenge me, ensuring that I'm constantly evolving and staying ahead in my field.

This practice of mental exercise goes beyond just gaining knowledge; it's about developing a growth mindset. A growth mindset has allowed me to view challenges not as obstacles but as opportunities to learn and improve. This mindset has been instrumental in helping me navigate the complexities of the business world and in making informed, strategic decisions.

Incorporating mindset work into daily life doesn't have to be overwhelming. It can start with simple habits like reading a few pages of a thought-provoking book each day or listening to a podcast that challenges your thinking. The key is consistency and intentionality. Here are some steps to enhance your mindset work:

- **Dedicate Time for Reading:** Set aside a specific time each day for reading, or listening, to books. Even just ten to fifteen minutes can make a significant difference. Choose books that inspire you, teach new concepts, or offer different perspectives on life and business.
- **Listen to Educational Podcasts:** Incorporate educational podcasts into your routine, perhaps during your commute or while exercising. Look for podcasts that challenge your thinking and offer insights into different areas of personal and professional growth. One of my all-time favorites is Ed Mylett's podcast.
- **Journal for Reflection and Growth:** Start a daily or weekly journaling practice. Use this as a space to reflect on your learnings, set goals, and ponder challenges and successes. Journaling can be a powerful tool for self-reflection and clarification of thoughts.
- **Engage in Thought-Provoking Conversations:** Seek out and engage in conversations with individuals who challenge you intellectually. This could be through networking events, professional groups, or even social settings.
- **Watch Informative Videos:** Regularly watch videos that offer educational content, such as TED Talks, documentaries, or

industry-specific seminars.
This audio-visual learning can be both engaging and a powerful tool for expanding your understanding of various subjects.

Remember, the goal of mindset work is to create a habit of continuous learning and intellectual growth. It's a habit that has profoundly impacted my life, allowing me to overcome personal challenges and achieve success in my career.

Habit #3: Doing Things That Move the Needle

In the quest for success, identifying and focusing on actions that "move the needle" is crucial. This concept is about prioritizing and dedicating time to tasks that have a significant impact on your goals. The first step is to discern what truly drives progress, then allocate your time accordingly.

In my career, especially in the earlier stages, taking practical steps meant being proactive and strategic with both my time and my effort. It often involved picking up the phone to actively call people scheduled for later in the month to ask if I could move those appointments up. A lot of other advisors would sit around and wait, but a sense of urgency drove my daily routine. If plans fell through, I didn't let the day go to waste. I quickly filled it with productive activities, such as rearranging schedules to keep the momentum or meeting clients.

Asking for referrals was also a crucial part of my strategy. I frequently reached out to existing clients, suggesting a quick visit to share an idea or seeking new connections through their networks. This proactive approach to expanding my client base helped me maximize every opportunity to grow.

Beyond these specific actions, establishing disciplined habits and routines was foundational. This included maintaining a consistent practice of reaching out, helping people recognize their needs, and being courageous in prospecting new clients. These activities, while seemingly simple, are like the small hinges that swing big doors. Their collective impact over time has been a significant contributor to building and sustaining a successful practice.

Here are some practical steps to ensure you're investing your time and energy in tasks that make a real difference:

- **Prioritize Your Tasks:** Begin each day by identifying the most critical tasks that will contribute significantly to your goals. Use a simple prioritization method, like the Eisenhower Box, to categorize tasks based on their urgency and importance. This helps in focusing your efforts on what truly matters.
- **Set Clear, Measurable Goals:** Define what success looks like for each major task or project. Having specific, measurable goals gives you a target to aim for and makes it

easier to recognize which actions are most vital in reaching these goals.
- **Limit Distractions:** As much as you can, create an environment conducive to focused work. This might mean turning off notifications, setting specific hours for checking emails, or creating a workspace that minimizes interruptions. By reducing distractions, you increase your ability to concentrate on high-impact tasks.
- **Regularly Review and Adjust:** Set aside time each week to review what you've accomplished and what's pending. This reflection allows you to adjust your plan so you can stay on track with activities that align with your objectives.
- **Learn to Delegate:** Understand that not everything needs your direct involvement. Delegate tasks that can be handled by others, freeing up your time for activities that only you can do and that have the most significant impact on your goals.
- **Cultivate a Sense of Urgency:** Treat your time as a precious resource. Develop a habit of acting with urgency, not haste, which means deliberately and swiftly taking steps toward your goals.

By adopting these strategies, you will be making certain that your tasks directly contribute to your success.

Habit #4: Joint Partnerships

In my career, the value of forming strategic partnerships has been immeasurable. These collaborations have not only accelerated my business growth but also broadened my perspective and skill set. One story that stands out in particular is my partnership with a colleague in the industry, whom I'll call Alex.

Alex and I came from different backgrounds, but we shared a common vision and work ethic. Our partnership began on a project that required a blend of our unique strengths. I brought to the table my expertise in client relationships and sales strategy, while Alex contributed his extensive knowledge in financial planning and analysis. Together, we were able to offer a comprehensive service that neither of us could have provided alone.

This partnership taught me a lot about the power of synergy. There were challenges, of course. We had to learn to communicate effectively, align our goals, and sometimes compromise to find the best solutions for our clients. But the effort was worth it. Our combined efforts led to successful outcomes that surpassed our individual capabilities.

One particular case with a major client demonstrated the strength of our partnership. We were faced with a complex financial situation that required both creative strategy and meticulous planning. Through our collaborative efforts, we were able to devise a solution that not only satisfied the client but also set a new standard for our service offerings. This experience was a testament to the fact that when you bring together different skills and perspectives, the potential for success is exponentially increased.

From this partnership, I learned the importance of choosing the right collaborators. Finding someone with complementary skills is important, but equally important is finding someone with shared values, mutual respect, and a joint commitment to excellence. Effective partnerships are built on trust, open communication, and a clear understanding of each other's roles and expectations.

In summary, embracing joint partnerships has been a key factor in my success. It's about recognizing that you can achieve more together than you can alone.

For anyone looking to expand their business or enhance their service offerings, I highly recommend exploring strategic collaborations. The right partnership can open doors to new opportunities and lead to achievements beyond your individual capacity. Here are some practical steps to get started:

- **Identify Potential Partners:** Look for individuals or organizations that complement your strengths and can fill in your gaps. Consider partners who share

similar values and goals but bring different skills or resources to the table.
- **Establish Clear Communication:** Open, honest, and frequent communication is vital. From the outset, discuss expectations, goals, and how you plan to handle disagreements. This foundation will help ensure a smooth partnership.
- **Set Shared Goals:** Define what success looks like for your partnership. Having shared objectives will keep both parties aligned and focused on common outcomes.
- **Develop a Formal Agreement:** Draft a partnership agreement that outlines roles, responsibilities, profit sharing, and other operational details. This formal arrangement can prevent misunderstandings and conflicts in the future.
- **Regularly Evaluate the Partnership:** Regularly assess how the partnership is performing compared to your goals. Be open to feedback and willing to make adjustments as needed.

Remember, the most successful partnerships are those where both parties benefit and grow. By taking a strategic approach to forming collaborations, you can significantly enhance the scope and impact of your business.

Embracing Transformative Habits

As we wrap up this chapter, I want to emphasize the transformative power of these four habits: exercise, cultivating a growth mindset, doing things that move the needle, and forming strategic partnerships. Personally, each of these practices has propelled me toward greater achievements and a more fulfilling life. But more importantly, these habits are accessible to anyone willing to commit to them.

Exercise and a growth mindset lay the foundation for personal well-being and resilience. They prepare you both physically and mentally to tackle the challenges and seize the opportunities that come your way. Prioritizing tasks that move the needle ensures that your efforts are aligned with your goals, maximizing the impact of your hard work. And, as my story with Alex shows, partnerships can amplify your strengths, mitigate your weaknesses, and lead to results that surpass individual efforts.

I encourage you, as you move forward in your own journey, to incorporate these habits into your daily routine. Start small if you need to, but start. The journey to success is not a sprint; it's a marathon. And it's the consistent, daily practices that will keep you on track and help you cross the finish line. Remember, the power to change your life lies in the actions you take each day.

FORCE FOR GOOD
MAKING A DIFFERENCE
THROUGH GENEROSITY

IN MY YOUNGER YEARS, like many, I was intensely focused on my own identity, career, and future as a provider. This self-absorption is common, as we often concentrate solely on our own success and achievements.

However, as I grew, both personally and spiritually, I began to see the importance of shifting focus from myself to others. I came to the belief that if we are blessed with fortune, be it skills, resources, or knowledge, we should consider helping improve others' situations.

This shift in perspective taught me the act of giving is far more rewarding than any financial success. In fact, the ability to make a meaningful impact in the lives of others—that is true success.

Appreciating the Generosity of Others

When we stop to think about how many people have helped us in our lives, it likely won't take long before we have quite a list. In my own life I think of:

- Mia, my grandmother
- My parents
- My brother, Tom
- Mrs. Jones, one of my first teachers
- Charles Lewis
- The police officer who helped me when I hit rock bottom
- All my friends in AA
- My employers
- My Northwestern Mutual colleagues
- Jack Musgrave and Fred Palmer
- My clients

If I took the time to list every individual, it would include hundreds of people!

And it's not just the number of people who have helped; it's the generosity of each person. Some of the folks in the above list have given me the equivalent of thousands of dollars, and more time and energy than I can even fathom.

Reflecting on the wealth of kindness and generosity I've received inspires me to engage in acts of giving myself.

Little Things That Make a Big Difference

When we think about the possibility of giving to others, our first thought might be, "Well, what can I give?" The real question is whether we're truly attentive to those around us. If we have been fortunate in certain aspects of our lives, are we willing to extend that fortune to others, to improve their situations with little acts of kindness? Being an encourager and a helper, making even a small difference in someone's life, is incredibly rewarding.

Love, I believe, is the underlying theme in all this—loving people for who they are and being mindful of opportunities to make subtle differences. In the past, if I did something nice, like buying someone a meal, I might have shared that story all day, but it was more about me than about the act of giving. Now I see the value in performing these acts quietly, letting them be moments between me and God.

Consider simple acts like noticing an elderly person in a grocery store who is carefully selecting items based on price. Telling the checker to add their groceries to your bill can make a significant difference. Though they may initially refuse out of pride, insisting gently shows respect and care. It's not always about financial help either. It can be as simple as helping someone put their groceries in their car or holding the door open for them. Small things like a smile, a look in the eye, can allow you to be a force for good in everyday situations.

These actions, seemingly minor, can have a profound impact. They are ways of showing love and kindness in a world that often overlooks such gestures. It's about being present and attentive, looking for those small opportunities where we can bring a bit of light and ease into someone else's life. By doing so, we not only enrich others' experiences but also find a deeper sense of purpose and joy in our own lives.

Not Always Easy

Giving isn't always easy. One particular day has stayed with me vividly. I was driving, and there, in the middle of the street, was a sight that caught me off guard. A poor man, seemingly in distress, was convulsing. The cold was biting, and I couldn't help but notice he was without shoes, which made the scene even more heart-wrenching.

I could sense he was in a bad place, possibly influenced by drugs, but that didn't lessen the gravity of his situation. It was a moment that required compassion, a moment where human kindness could have made all the difference. I watched as a few people pulled over, quickly springing into action and calling for an ambulance.

But my reaction was different. I hesitated; a sense of fear held me back. Despite my nature, which often leans toward helping, I found myself paralyzed in that moment. I didn't rush out of my car to wrap him in a warm blanket or check if he was okay. Even though it was clear he was struggling and needed help, my apprehension took over.

That day, witnessing the man in distress and not acting when I could have, left me with a sense of guilt, a feeling that I should have done more. It's a feeling many of us encounter at some point—the regret of inaction in moments when our conscience nudges us to step forward.

If you've ever felt a sense of guilt like this, here's my advice: Let it go. It's essential to release the shame and the narrative we tell ourselves about such moments. Recognize that any change in behavior, even if it's minor or gradual, is still progress.

Even simply reflecting on your actions, or in some cases inaction, is a step forward. It signifies your desire to do better, to be more present and responsive in the future.

At the end of the day, everyone wants to feel appreciated and help others. But we live in a world that often focuses more on self-absorption than on truly helping. This realization is important. It reminds us that any shift toward a more compassionate, action-oriented approach, no matter how small, is valuable. We don't have to be perfect or "100 percent in" right from the start. What matters is our willingness to grow, to be a little bit better each time, and to gradually align our actions with our intentions of helping and supporting others.

True Success

It's easy to think of generosity as just a nice gesture, an optional add-on to our lives. But this view fails to grasp the profound impact and fulfillment generosity brings. Giving back has been way more fulfilling than depositing a big check into my bank account. Sure, big checks are nice, but in and of themselves, they don't accomplish much. It's the use of our time, talent, and treasure for the benefit of others that truly enriches our lives.

Throughout my journey, both personal and professional, I've realized that true success isn't measured by financial gains or material acquisitions. Instead, it's found in the acts of giving and the meaningful connections we forge in our lives. The most rewarding experiences haven't been about closing big deals or accumulating wealth; they've been moments of sharing what I have with those in need. Whether it's speaking a kind word, giving a helping hand, or sharing resources, these acts of generosity have brought a richness to my life that far surpasses any financial metric.

True success involves looking beyond our own needs and considering how we can contribute to the well-being of others. It's about understanding that our greatest achievements come not from what we accumulate for ourselves, but from what we give to others. This giving doesn't just change the lives of the recipients; it transforms us, offering a deeper sense of satisfaction and fulfillment.

The joy of seeing someone's life improved because of a simple act of kindness, the sense of connection that comes from helping others, and the personal growth that follows—these are the true measures of success. They represent a richness of life that no amount of money can buy.

Tips for Being Generous

Here are practical tips to help cultivate this valuable trait:

- **Reflect on Generosity Received:** Take fifteen minutes to list as many people as you can think of who have been generous to you. Reflecting on these acts of kindness can inspire you to pay it forward.
- **Anticipate Opportunities for Kindness:** As you plan your day, think about your schedule and the interactions you'll have. Look for opportunities to incorporate small acts of generosity, whether it's a compliment, a helping hand, or a moment of encouragement.
- **Listen Actively and Offer Help:** Pay attention to those around you. Offering support, giving advice, or simply being there for someone can be a profound act of kindness.

- **Embrace Random Acts of Kindness:** Small, unexpected gestures like paying for someone's coffee or leaving a positive note can make a significant difference in someone's day.
- **Volunteer Your Time:** Giving your time to causes or community events is a valuable form of generosity. Even a few hours can make a big impact.
- **Utilize Your Skills for Good:** Think about how your talents can help others. Whether it's mentoring, helping with a project, or providing pro bono services, your skills are valuable.
- **Consider a Generosity Goal:** What if you allowed yourself to think bigger about your capacity for generosity? While you might not be able to fund an entire project like an orphanage in Africa right now, start dreaming about a cause where you can make a significant impact. Setting a long-term generosity goal gives you something to work toward and can shape your actions and decisions in a meaningful way.

Incorporating these practices into your life can help you embrace and spread generosity in ways far more significant than you can imagine. Remember, it's not about the size of the gesture but the heart behind it and the positive impact it creates.

GROUNDED IN GRACE
THE ROLE OF FAITH IN MY LIFE

AS I REFLECT ON THE JOURNEY of my life, one aspect stands out as a cornerstone of my being—my faith. This chapter is a testament to how faith in God has played a transformative role in my life, particularly in my path to sobriety and personal growth.

From a young age, I always believed in God. I saw Him as a friend and a comforter, a presence that brought peace and solace. Throughout my life, faith was a constant, a familiar comfort, even when I wasn't actively pursuing a spiritual path.

However, it was during the lowest points of my life that my faith took on a new, profound meaning. Hitting rock bottom was a pivotal moment when I realized my recovery needed something beyond human capabilities. It was at this point that I truly turned to God, understanding that my sobriety was a gift from Him. I start and end each day with prayer, a practice that grounds me in gratitude and reminds me of the journey I've traveled with God's guidance.

Don't get me wrong, my life isn't perfect. Like anyone's journey, it has its ups and downs. But what remains paramount is maintaining a positive attitude and unshakable faith in God, trusting that everything will work itself out.

My faith isn't just about religious practice; it's about living a life that reflects the principles of love, compassion, and encouragement—attributes I associate with being God-like. As a Christian, I have chosen to walk the path with Jesus as my Lord and Savior, finding in His teachings the essence of these virtues.

I believe in showing love and kindness in a world often consumed by self-interest. Being close to God, for me, means embodying these qualities, being present for others, and extending a helping hand. It's about living a life that's joyous, free, and grounded in the values I hold dear.

I understand that faith can be a delicate subject, especially in a world with diverse beliefs and experiences. My approach is not about imposing my beliefs but about living in a way that hopefully inspires others to seek their path to fulfillment.

As I look back and see where I've come from and where I am today, I can't help but feel an immense sense of gratitude. God has blessed me enormously, in more ways than I can count. And it's this gratitude that propels me to keep growing, to keep seeking ways to get closer to God, and to be a better human being.

As we reach the end of this journey together, I hope this book has not just told my story, but also encouraged you to embrace your own journey with courage and optimism. May you find strength in your challenges, joy in your achievements, and above all, a deeper connection with the passions and values that guide your life. Thank you for walking this path with me, and may your future be filled with growth, discovery, and fulfillment!

ABOUT THE AUTHOR

CHRISTOPHER O. KOON is a distinguished figure in the insurance and financial services industry, with a career spanning over twenty-five years at Northwestern Mutual, a Fortune 100 company. His expertise in providing world-class insurance services and internationally recognized investment products has earned him a reputation for dependability and success in his field. Chris's journey to the top wasn't without challenges. Overcoming dyslexia and early educational hurdles, he harnessed his struggles to fuel his professional drive. His remarkable achievements include being a Lifetime Member of the Million Dollar Round Table and ranking in the top 1 percent of industry producers. Chris lives in St. Louis with his wife, Lisa Rose, and their three children, Berkley, Ava, and Gunnar.

CONNECT WITH CHRIS KOON!

For speaking inquiries, personal consultations, or to simply share your thoughts and experiences, Chris Koon welcomes you to reach out.

INSTAGRAM: @thekooner1
EMAIL: Chris.Koon@nm.com
WEBSITE: www.chris-koon.com

Chris looks forward to hearing from you and continuing the conversation beyond the pages of this book.